OFFICERS & SOLDIERS

FRENCH ARMY
1941-1945

Forces Françaises Libres (*Free French Forces*), Forces
Françaises de l'Intérieur (*Internal Resistance forces*),
Army of Liberation

André JOUINEAU

Organisation charts by François VAUVILLIER
Translated from the French by Alan McKAY

Histoire & Collections

THE FRENCH ARMY, AFTER THE DEFEAT

The Armistice Army and the Chantiers de jeunesse

In order to get people to forget the June 1940 defeat, the Vichy Government started reforming the army which the occupier had been good enough to let it keep.

From 1941 onwards, the Army brought in changes in the cut of the uniform; new insignia appeared using the French flag with a distinctive sign for each military arm, as did embroidered escutcheons. Each regiment was attributed an embroidered escutcheon.

The Chantiers de jeunesse (Youth Work Sites) were created in 1942 to "occupy and instruct" the classes that could not be mobilised. A special uniform was designed for them with embroidered insignia and special ranks.

The Free French Forces

In June 1940, Britain took in a variety of French troops comp[..] sing mainly men from the Narvik Expeditionary Forces, those w[..] had managed to scrounge a lift on British ships during Operati[..] Dynamo (the evacuation from the Dunkirk pocket), sailors and [..] few pilots. The soldiers now had to make a choice: be sent back [..] France or rally General de Gaulle who, in his 18 June speech, call[..] all men to continue the fight.

From July onwards, all the soldiers who had rallied General [..] Gaulle under the name of *Forces Françaises Libres* (Free Fren[..] Forces) were completely re-equipped by the English with battledres[..] equipment and weapons. The Free French were allowed to ke[..] their headgear, insignia, ranks markings and specialisations, and t[..]

Army of the Armistice in France, North Africa and Levant

FORMATION	HQ	INFANTRY	CAVALRY	ARTILLERY
I - IN SOUTHERN FRANCE *(Summer 1940 to November 1942; disbanded after the German invasion)*				
1er GDM	Avignon (General Olry)			
7e DM	Bourg-en-Bresse	65e, 151e RI, 4e (1er, 2e, 10e) DBCP	5e RD	61e RA
14e DM	Lyon	153e, 159e RI, 3e (6e, 13e, 27e) DBCA	11e RC	2e RAM
15e DM	Marseille	43e RIA, 21e RIC, 173e BI Corse, 2e (20e, 24e, 25e) DBCA	12e RC	10e RAC
16e DM	Montpellier	8e, 51e RI, 2e RIC	3e RD	15e RA
1re Brigade de Cavalerie *(horse Rgts, attached to 1er GDM)*			1er, 7e RCh	
2e GDM	Royat (General Réquin)			
9e DM	Châteauroux	1er, 27e, 32e RI	8e RC	72e RA
12e DM	Limoges	26e, 41e RI, 1re (8e, 16e, 30e) DBCP	6e RC	35e RA
13e DM	Limoges	5e, 92e, 152e RI	8e RD	4e RA
17e DM	Toulouse	18e, 23e, 150e RI	2e RD	24e RA
2e Brigade de Cavalerie *(horse Rgts, attached to 2e GDM)*			2e, 3e RH	
II - IN NORTH AFRICA *(in January 1941; several changes occurred after the Syrian campaign)*				
DTA[1]	Alger	1er RZ, 1er, 9e RTA, 13e RTS	5e RCA, 1er RSA	65e RAA
DTO[1]	Oran	2e RZ, 2e, 6e RTA, 1er REI	2e RCA, 2e RSA	66e RAA
DTC[1]	Constantine	3e RZ, 3e, 7e RTA, 15e RTS	3e RCA, 3e RSA	67e RAA
Reserves in Algeria		5e RTA, 8e RTT		68e RAA
Reserves in Tunisia		4e RZ, 4e RTT, 43e RIC	4e RCA, 4e RST	62e RAA
Morocco	Fez	11e RTA, 4e, 5e RTM, 3e REI, I/6e RTS	1er REC	63e RAA
	Meknès	7e RTM, 3e REI (elements)	3e RSM	64e RAA
	Casablanca	1er, 6e RTM, RICM, 6e RTS	1er RCA	RACM (3 gr.)
	Marrakech	2e RTM, 2e REI	4e RSM	RACM (1 gr.)
Reserves in Morocco		3e, 8e RTM		
New cavalry units created in Africa in 1941		8e, 9e RCA, 10e, 11e, 12e GAPCA (groupes autonomes portés de chas. d'Af.), 2e RMSA		
III - IN LEVANT *(at the beginning of the Syrian campaign, May 1941)*				
Lebanon		22e, 29e RTA, II/16e RTT, 6e REI	6e RCA, 4e GrST	RAC Levant
Syria		I+II/24e RMIC, 1er, 2e, 3e BCL*I+III/16e RTT, III/29e RTA, V/1er RTM, III/24e RMIC, 17e RTS, 8 Syrian Btns* + 3 Meharists Cos*	8e GrSA, 7e RCA, 1er RSM, 4 Line + 6 Druzes, + 8 Tcherkess Sqdns	1er RAMLevant, Aleppo Group*

1. Division territoriale d'Alger, d'Oran and de Constantine. * Local forces from the 'Troupes spéciales du Levant' (BCL = Lebanese Chasseurs Battalion).

...oice of where to put them. To this was added a shoulder flash with ...RANCE" on it.

The *Forces Navales Françaises Libres* (FNFL – Free French Naval ...rces) were created in July 1940. The sailors retained their insignia ...d their uniforms to which they added the FNFL insignia. The *Fusi-...rs-Marins* (Marines) adopted British uniform and equipment but ...pt their headdress.

The first French Air Force pilots who reached England were incorpo-...ted into the English squadrons after passing their RAF pilot's qualifi-...tions. They kept some of the French distinctives which were ratified ...en the autonomous fighter and bomber groups were set up.

...eclerc's Column

...Operating to begin with in North Africa, most of the troops in the ...lumn were colonial. They held onto their French uniforms from ...fore the Armistice and added the FFL insignia or the *Croix de ...rraine*, the symbol rallying all the Free French.

...Some of the units were re-equipped by the British. The general ...pression these troops gave was very much that of the "Army of ...rica".

The French Army in North Africa

...Until November 1942 the French troops in North Africa were un-...r the orders of the Vichy Government. After the Americans landed ... North Africa, priority was given to rearming them so that they

Main Free French units, 1940-1941

TROOPS RAISED IN GREAT BRITAIN, June-July 40	
14e DBLE (13e again from Nov. 40) (also known as 1er BLE — bataillon de légion étrangère)	c.900 Legionnaires from Norway
1re CCFL (cie de chars de la France Libre)	12 Hotchkiss H 39 tanks from Norway
BVF (bataillon de volontaires français) (became BCC — bataillon de chasseurs de Camberley. Disbanded on 8 Dec. 40. Became Cadets de la France Libre, a cadre for FF officers and NCOs)	c.220 chasseurs and Breton volunteers
1er BFM (bataillon de fusiliers marins) (infantry, then AA unit from early 1941. A 2e BFM was created during that year. Sept. 43, 1er BFM became 1er RFM, armoured recce Rgt of 1er DMI)	c.400 sailors organized as a land unit
1re CIA (future SAS French Squadron)	c.20 paras
+ small detachments of artillery, engineers, signals and services	
TROOPS FROM LEVANT, June-July 40 (initially known as détachement français en Egypte, then GVFE — groupement des volontaires français d'Egypte)	
1er BIM (bataillon d'infanterie de marine; (the 1er BIM fought with the British 7th Arm.Div. from Sept. 40 to May 41)	c.470, from 24e RIC
ESM (escadron de spahis marocains)	42, from 1er RSM (future RMSM)
TROOPS FROM BLACK AFRICA	
BM 1 (1er bataillon de marche)	c.800 Senegalese (Brazzaville, 29 Aug. 40)
BM 2 (2e bataillon de marche)	c.750 Senegalese (Bangui, Nov. 40)
BM 3 (3e bataillon de marche)	c.800 Senegalese (Chad, Dec. 40)
BM 4 (4e bataillon de marche). (followed in 1941 by further BMs of similar strength)	c.800 Senegalese (Cameroun, Dec. 40)
RTST (rgt de tirailleurs sénégalais du Tchad; These Chadian troops formed Leclerc's raiding columns	469 French, 5 664 locals: Senegalese plus c.400 Tuareg camel troopers from the GN (groupes nomades) of Ennedi, Borku and Tibesti
TROOPS FROM TAHITI AND NEW CALEDONIA	
BP 1 (1er bataillon du Pacifique (BP 1 became BIMP after being amalgamated with 1er BIM in Summer 42)	c.600 European and locals (Noumea, May 41)

Free French Brigades and Divisions 1940 à 1943

FORMATION	GENERAL OR CO	INFANTRY (BTN LEVEL)	RECCE.	TANKS	ARTILLERY	CAMPAIGNS AND OTHER COMMENTS
MAIN BODY OF FREE FRENCH TROOPS (included in the Order of Battle of the British and Commonwealth forces)						
In September 1940						
1re Brigade de Légion française (1re BLF)	de Gaulle	14e DBLE, 1er BFM	—	1re CCFL	1 Section	Section Shipped on 15 Sept. 40 from UK to Dakar, then diverted to Cameroun after failure of Operation Menace
which became (from 21 October 1940)						
Brigade française d'Orient (BFO)	(Col.) Monclar	1er BLE, 1er BFM, BM 2, 3	(1er ESM)*	1re CCFL	1 Section	At full strength in late Dec. 40, for the Eritrean campaign
which became (from 11 April 1941)						
1re Division d'infanterie des FFL	Legentilhomme	1re Bde: 1er BLE, BM 1, BM 2 / 2e Bde: 1er BIM, BM 3, BM 4	1er ESM Sudanese Sqdn	1re CCFL	2 Batteries 1er BFM (AA)	Syrian campaign, June-July 41
The 1re DIFFL was disbanded in Syria on 20 Aug. 41, to form 2 new DLIs (divisions légères d'infanterie) which did not see service as such, but were modified in Dec. 41 as follows:						
which became (from 23 December 1941)						
Corps français du *Western Desert*	de Larminat					Known as 'Groupe français libre' from 4 March 42
1re Brigade française libre (indépendante)	Kœnig	2e, 3e BLE, 1er BIM, BM 2, BP 1	—*	—*	1er RA, 1er BFM (AA)	Libyan campaign 1942 (Bir Hacheim)
2e Brigade française libre (indépendante)	Cazaud	1er BLE, BM 3 (then 5), 4, 11			1 Battery	Libyan campaign 1942
A 3e Brigade française libre was also created in the Levant, May 42, with BM 6, 7, 9. It did not see action, as its role was to maintain the French presence there						
Colonne volante (Free French Flying column)			GR 1, GR 2 1er RMSM in sept. 42	1er CCFL		
which became (from 1st February 1943)						
1re Division française libre (1re DFL) (1re DFL initial strength with 2 Bdes: 10,234)	Kœnig	1re Bde: 13e (1er, 2e) DBLE, BIMP / 2e Bde: BM 4, BM 5, BM 11 / 4e Bde*: BM 21, BM 22, BM 24	(1er RMSM, 1er CCFL)*	1er RA, 2e RAC		Tunisian campaign from 6 April 4. Then, the 1re DFL was sent to Syria (June 43) from French Somaliland.

...nne Leclerc' (used as a separate, solely French force, until it reached the British VIIIth Army in Tripoli, 23 Jan. 43), then 'Force L' from 12 February 43. The Leclerc Column was initially c.460 men strong (raid on Kufra, Jan.-March 41), then c.900 men (first Fezzan campaign, ...-March 42). For the conquest of the Fezzan (Dec. 42-Jan. 43), it started with 2,758 men. After his victory in the Fezzan, Leclerc drove northwards to Libya and Tripoli. During the Tunisian campaign, the FF Flying Column was incorporated into Force L (12 March). Leclerc's ...es, officially referred to as '2e DFL' from 12 May, were withdrawn in June 43 from Tunisia to Tripolitania.

French Army Order of Battle, Tunisian Campaign, November 1942-May 1943

FORMATION	GENERAL	INFANTRY (BTN LEVEL)	CAVALRY	ARTILLERY	CAMPAIGNS AND OTHER COMMENTS
DAF	Juin				Détachement d'armée français, created 19 Nov. 42
CSTT	Barré	4e RMZT, 4e RTT, III/43e RIC (1 btn)	4e RCA, 4e RST	62e RAA	Tunisian Command (partly interned in Bizerta, 19 Nov. 42
19e CA	Koeltz			63e RAA (1 By)	Formed 16 Nov., known as CAF (French Army Corps) from Febr. 43
DMC	Welvert († 10-4) then Schwartz	3e RZ, 1er, 2e, 3e, 7e, 9e RTA, 4e RTT, 7e RTM, 15e RTS, 2e GTM	3e, 5e RCA, 3e RSA, 4e RST	62e, 64e, 65e, 66e, 67e RAA, RACM, RACL	Joined 19e CA on 16 Nov. Disbanded 30 Apr. 43
BLM	du Vigier then St-Didier		Tks and motor sqdns : 2e, 5e, 9e RCA (elts)	68e RAA (elts)	Joined 19e CA on 18 Nov. Disbanded 28 Feb. 43
Gpt Aurès	de Goutel		3e, 6e RSA		Joined 19e CA on 24 Nov., incorporated into FSEA or 18 Feb. 43
DMA	Deligne then Conne	3e RZ, 1er, 9e RTA, 2e GTM	5e RCA, 1er RSA	65e RAA	Joined 19e CA on 25 Nov. 42
1re DMM	Mathenet	29e RTA, 7e RTM, II/1er, 3e REI, 1er GTM	1er REC	1er RMAM	Formed Dec. 42, joined CSTT, then 19e CA on 29 Jan.
DMO	Boissau	2e, 6e RTA, 15e RTS, 1er REI		62e, 66e, 68e RAA	Late formation, joined CAF on 29 April 43
FES	Delay	Meharist Coys, 1er REI (Saharan Coy), etc.		Foreign Legion Batts	Formed 15 Nov. 42, incorporated in FSEA on 18 Feb.4
FSEA	Boissau	FES + II/16e RTT, 3e REI, I/13e RTS	3e, 9e, 12e RCA (élém.) 1er, 3e RSA (élém.)	Foreign Legion Batts	Formed 18 Feb. 43 with FES and Gpt des Aurès, then disbanded 12 April 43
GBF	Le Coulteux		Tanks: 5e, 9e, 12e RCA (1 sqdn each), 1 US light tk Coy		Formed 13 April 43

French Army Order of Battle, Sept. 1943-May 1945 (formations from North Africa)

FORMATION	GENERAL	INFANTRY (BTN LEVEL)	RECCE	TANKS [1]	ARTILLERY	CAMPAIGNS AND OTHER COMMENTS
ORDER OF BATTLE UNTIL SUMMER1944						
ARMIES AND ARMY CORPS						
CEF (aka Détachement d'armée A)	Juin	1er, 3e, 4e GTM attached	—	7e, 8e RCA	64e RAA, RACL	Italy (November 1943-July 44)
1re Armée (Armée B until Sept. 44)	de Lattre de Tassigny	2e GTM	—	2e RD	—	France 1944-45, Germany, Austria 1945
1er CA	Martin then Bethouart (sept. 44)					Corsica (Sept. 43), Elba (June 44).
2e CA (created Aug. 43)	de Larminat then de Monsabert				I, II/RAC	Campaigns: France, Germany, Austria
INFANTRY DIVISIONS						
1re DMI (div. motorisée d'infanterie, ex-1re DFL)	Brosset then Garbay (nov. 1944)	1re Bde: 1er, 2e BLE, 22e BMNA. 2e Bde: BM 4, BM 5, BM 11. 4e Bde: BIMP, BM 21, BM 24 + 11e Cuirassiers (ex-FFI) as an infantry regiment (Sept.44-Feb.45)	1er RFM	8e RCA[1]	1er RA	Italy (Apr.-July 44), France, Germany
2e DIM (division d'infanterie marocaine)	Dody puis Carpentier (sept. 44) and de Linarès (avril 1945).	4e, 5e, 8e RTM. LAll three RTMs became mixed (2 Moroccan, 1 Algerian Btn each) in August 44. 8e RTM replaced by 151e RI in March 45. 20e BCP (ex-20e BCA FFI) attached in March 45.	3e RSM	8e RCA[1]	63e RAA	Italy (Nov. 43-July 44), France, Germany, Austria
3e DIA (division d'infanterie algérienne)	de Goislard then de Monsabert	3e, 7e RTA, 4e RTT. 7e RTA replaced by 49e RI (ex-CF Pommiès) in Feb. 45.	3e RSAR	7e RCA	67e RAA	Italy (Dec. 43-July 44), France, Germany
4e DMM (division marocaine de montagne)	Sevez then Guillaume (sept. 1944) then de Hesdin (déc. 1944)	1er, 2e, 6e RTM 2e RTM replaced by 1er RTA in July 1944; 1er RTA replaced by 27e RI in Feb. 45.	4e RSM		69e RAM	Corsica (Sept. 43), Italy (Feb.-July 44), France, Germany
9e DIC (division d'infanterie coloniale)	Blaizot then Magnan, then Morlière (dec. 44), then Valluy (march 1945).	4e, 6e, 13e RTS. All three Senegalese regiments became 21e, 6e and 23e RIC respectively with European personnel (ex-FFI) in Nov. 44.	RICM	RCCC)	RACM	Elba (June 44), Italy, France, Germany
ARMOURED DIVISIONS (DB = DIVISIONS BLINDÉES)						
1re DB	Touzet du Vigier then Sudre (december 1944)	Tanks: 2e RC, 2e, 5e RCA Infantry: 1re DBZ	3e RCA	9e RCA	68e RAA	France, Germany
2e DB (ex-2e DFL, ex-Leclerc Column)	Leclerc	Tanks: 12e RC, 12e RCA, 501e RCC Infantry: RMT	1er RMSM	RBFM	I/3e RAC, I/40e RANA, XI/64e RA	France (Normandy), Germany
5e DB	de Vernejoul then Schlesser (apr. 45)	Tanks: 1er RC, 1er, 6e RCA Inf.: RMLE	1er REC	11e RCA	62e RAA	France, Germany, Austria
Except 9e RCA, tank destroyer regiments did not belong organically to any formation, but were almost permanently allocated 'in support'. 8e RCA supported 2e DIM then from June 44 1re DMI.						
General reserve units. From North Africa: 4e, 9e RZ, 1er, 2e RSAR, 1er, 3e Gpt de Choc.						
From metropolitan soil: 19e BCP, 24e BCA, 2e Gpt de Choc.						

Key to new abbreviations
BMNA : bataillon de marche nord-africain
DBZ : demi-brigade de zouaves
RMLE : régiment de marche de la légion étrangère
RCCC : régiment colonial de chasseurs de chars
RBFM : régiment blindé de fusiliers marins
RSAR : régiment de spahis algériens de reconnaissance.

Preliminary notes: as many changes occurred during the campaign, and as many units fought split among several divisions, this table does not reflect a fixed situation. Free French Forces (1ᵉ DFL and Leclerc force) also fought in Tunisia. See Table p. 5.

Key to new abbreviations (all other designations have been explained in Volume One)
CSTT: commandement supérieur des troupes de Tunisie / Tunisian Troops Command
DMC, DMA, DMO: division de marche de Constantine, d'Alger, d'Oran / Provisional division of Constantine, Algiers and Oran.
BLM: brigade légère mécanique / Light mechanized brigade (comprising 2 tank squadrons plus armoured cars, motorcycle combinations and motor squadrons)
DMM: division marocaine de montagne / Moroccan mountain division
GBF: groupement blindé français / French armoured group (mixture of Somua and Valentine tanks)
GTM: groupe de tabors marocains / Moroccan tabor group (roughly equivalent to an infantry regiment)
RMAM: régiment de marche d'artillerie du Maroc / Provisional artillery regiment of Morocco   FES : front est saharien / East Saharan front
FSEA : front du Sud est algérien / South East Algerian front

...uld confront the Afrika Korps coming from Tunisia. Their uniforms ...nd weapons gradually incorporated various articles from the Ame-can army uniform. For some time afterwards there was a delightful ...lend of items from the Armistice uniform, items from the French ...935 uniform, from the American uniform, and even some from the ...ritish uniform as and when the soldiers were re-equipped.

The new army from FFI and FTP

The national underground movement was at first limited to intel-gence gathering and only took part in military operations from ...942 onwards. It therefore had no arms and no uniforms except for a few of the officers who were former soldiers. In 1944 some elements from the Armistice army *"took to the Maquis"*, i.e. went underground, with their weapons and their baggage often accompanied by men from the Chantiers de jeunesse. The Underground had no qualms at all about taking material, equipment or even items of uniforms for themselves from the CDJ stores, or off the occupation army, making for very disparate, improvised uniforms whose only distinctive feature was a tricolour armband. They had to wait for the FFI to be incorporated into the regular army before a uniform appeared, usually handed over by the American army.

Like the 2ᵉ DB (2nd Armoured Division) re-equipped in England, the other French units became the responsibility of the Americans who supplied weapons, equipment and uniforms.

The French often held on to their traditional headgear and the metal regimental insignia. The French flag also appeared on their sleeves, with arm lozenges in the regimental colour with two braid stripes for the mainland (Metropolitan) regiments and three for the troops from Africa; and the marks of rank were above that, or on a flap held in place by buttons, on the front of the uniform.

Regiments dating back to the Armistice army kept their 1941-model escutcheon which disappeared in 1945.

FORMATION	GENERAL	INFANTRY (BTN LEVEL) (niveau du Btn)	RECCE.	ARTILLERY	CAMPAIGNS AND OTHER COMMENTS
	**5 - Main French formations raised on metropolitan soil from FFI units, 1944-1945**
DAAtl (Détachement d'armée de l'Atlantique)	de Larminat	4ᵉ RZ, 8ᵉ RTS, Rgt AEF-Somalie	13ᵉ RD		1 March 45 from Forces françaises de l'Ouest (FFO, created Oct. 44)
DAAlp (Détachement d'armée des Alpes)	Doyen	3ᵉ, 99ᵉ, 141ᵉ RIA, 29ᵉ RTA, 18ᵉ RTS		69ᵉ RAA	1 March 45 from Secteur des Alpes (created Oct. 44)
3ᵉ CA	Leclerc	—	4ᵉ RH	11ᵉ, 30ᵉ RA	28 Jan. 45. Formed from Feb. 45
	**INFANTRY DIVISIONS (in chronological order of reconstruction, prior to 8 May 45)**
19ᵉ DI	Borgnis-Desbordes	41ᵉ, 71ᵉ, 118ᵉ RI	19ᵉ RD	10ᵉ RA	6 Sept. 44 in Brittany. Fought in Lorient pocket
10ᵉ DI	Billotte	5ᵉ, 24ᵉ, 46ᵉ RI	18ᵉ RD	32ᵉ RA	1 Oct. 44. Fought in Alsace and in Atlantic pockets
27ᵉ DA (alpine)	Vallette d'Osia, then Molle (Feb. 45)	159ᵉ RIA, 5ᵉ (7ᵉ, 13ᵉ, 27ᵉ) DBCA (7ᵉ 6ᵉ, 11ᵉ, 15ᵉ) DBCA	5ᵉ RD	93ᵉ RAM	16 Nov. 44 as 1ᵉ DAFFI. Fought in the Alps
1ʳᵉ DI	Calliès then Bertrand	1ᵉʳ, 43ᵉ, 110ᵉ RI	12ᵉ RCh	15ᵉ RA	12 Dec. 44. Sent to Germany early May 45, did not see action
23ᵉ DI	D'Anselme puis Adeline	6ᵉ, 50ᵉ, 158ᵉ RI	18ᵉ RCh	2ᵉ RA	22 Jan. 45. Fought in Atlantic pockets (Royan-Aunis)
36ᵉ DI	Cazaud	14ᵉ, 18ᵉ, 57ᵉ RI	2ᵉ RH	24ᵉ RA	15 Feb. 45. Sent to the Alps, too late to see action
14ᵉ DI	Salan	35ᵉ, 152ᵉ RI, 3ᵉ (2ᵉ, 4ᵉ, 31ᵉ) DBCP	12ᵉ RD	4ᵉ RA	16 Feb. 45. Fought in Alsace and Germany
25ᵉ DI	Chomel	21ᵉ, 32ᵉ RI, 4ᵉ (1ᵉ, 5ᵉ, 17ᵉ) DBCP	1ᵉʳ RH	20ᵉ RA	22 Jan. 45. Formed April 45, fought in Saint Nazaire pocket
	**COLONIAL INFANTRY DIVISIONS (DCEO = division coloniale d'Extrême-Orient, intended for Far East and the reconquest of Indochina)**
1ʳᵉ DCEO	Nyo	16ᵉ, 18ᵉ RTS, Rgt AEF-Somalie	5ᵉ RC	10ᵉ RAC	16 Nov. 44. Did not see action, became 3ᵉ DIC in Aug. 45
2ᵉ DCEO	Astier de Villatte	2ᵉ Bde col. d'EO: 4ᵉ, 5ᵉ, 6ᵉ Bat. col. d'EO 3ᵉ Bde légion d'EO: 1ᵉʳ, 2ᵉ, 3ᵉ BLE d'EO	8ᵉ RCh Tks: 9ᵉ RD	7ᵉ RAC 8ᵉ RAC	1-27 Dec. 44. Did not see action, disbanded in June 45
	**ARMOURED DIVISION**
3ᵉ DB	de Langlade	Tanks: 4ᵉ, 11ᵉ RC, 13ᵉ RD Inf.: 1ʳᵉ (8ᵉ, 16ᵉ, 30ᵉ) DBCP	11ᵉ RCh TD: 6ᵉ RC	16ᵉ RA	1 May 45. Did not see action

Infantry regiments not part of a division (lines of communication, etc.): 23ᵉ, 26ᵉ, 33ᵉ, 39ᵉ, 42ᵉ, 48ᵉ, 51ᵉ, 65ᵉ, 67ᵉ, 94ᵉ, 95ᵉ, 106ᵉ, 117ᵉ, 121ᵉ, 129ᵉ, 134ᵉ, 137ᵉ, 146ᵉ; Jura and Swiss borders : 4ᵉ; DAATL : 8ᵉ, 13ᵉ, 34ᵉ, 38ᵉ, 91ᵉ, 92ᵉ 108ᵉ 114ᵉ, 150ᵉ; General reserves of 1ʳᵉ Armée : 60ᵉ, 80ᵉ, 81ᵉ 126ᵉ 131ᵉ; Pyrenees spanish borders :153ᵉ, 170ᵉ, 173ᵉ RIA.

The Generals

General (Major
General) wearing
campaign dress.

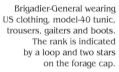

Brigadier-General wearing
US clothing, model-40 tunic,
trousers, gaiters and boots.
The rank is indicated
by a loop and two stars
on the forage cap.

Brigadier-General
wearing battle-dress
with epaulet rank loops.

Major-General wearing US
dress. He has kept
his Adrian helmet
with three stars and
is wearing Buckle Boots.

Lieutenant-General
wearing a US Mackinaw.

The Generals

Brigadier-General wearing a greatcoat, in French clothing.

Brigadier-General from the CEF *(Corps Expéditionnaire Français)* in Italy wearing US summer clothing.

General in the 1re Division Blindée (1st Armoured Division).

He is wearing a US model-39 tunic on which the buttons have been replaced. The rank markings are on a dark blue cloth triangle sewn onto the bottom of the sleeves US trousers and gaiters; the forage cap is in the colours of the Cuirassiers, with a Major-General's three stars.

Major-General from the CEF (*Corps Expéditionnaire Français* – French Expeditionary Corps) in Italy wearing the Goumiers' jellaba over a US uniform and his forage cap is in the traditional colours of the Goumiers.

Major-General wearing a US model-39 greatcoat and US equipment with a Colt 45, US trousers and Buckle Boots.

The Generals

Brigadier-General
wearing French clothing
and a forage cap.

Major-General wearing
British clothing.

General commanding
an armoured division.
He is wearing the Model-35
armoured troops helmet with
his marks of rank,
a Mackinaw on which
a 1941-type escutcheon
bearing the armoured troops'
insignia and his Brigadier's
stars has been sewn.

Major-General
in Italy in around 1942.

Lieutenant-General wearing
heavy cotton clothing in Italy
in around 1944.

The Military Colleges

Cadet (Cherchell Academy) wearing manoeuvres dress in around 1943.

Cadet (Cherchell Academy) wearing parade dress in around 1944.

Cadet wearing canvas dress of Sergeant in the 43ᵉ Transmissions Regiment (Signals).

Free French Cadet in Cumberley, Great Britain, 1941.

Cadet wearing manoeuvres dress.

FRANCE LIBRE

The Forces Françaises de l'Intérieur

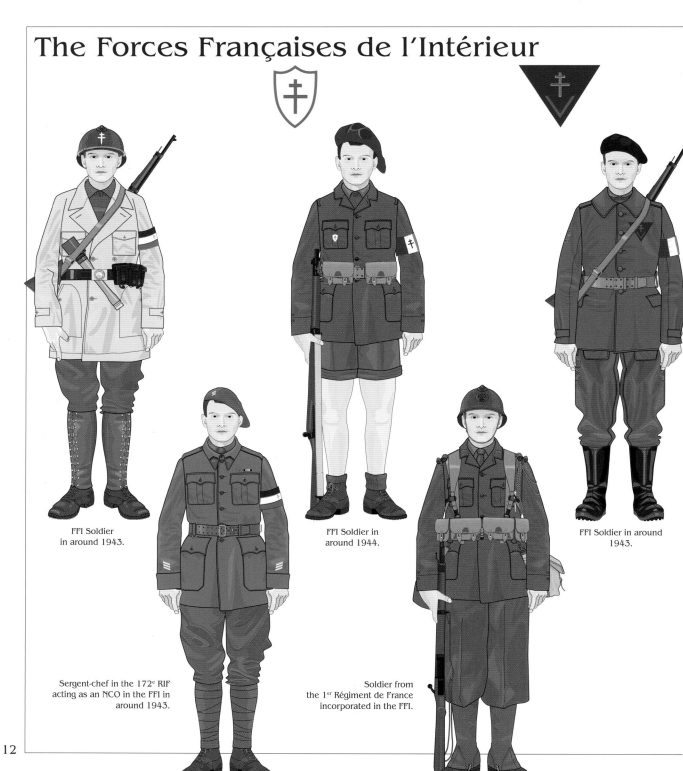

FFI Soldier
in around 1943.

FFI Soldier in
around 1944.

FFI Soldier in around
1943.

Sergent-chef in the 172ᵉ RIF
acting as an NCO in the FFI in
around 1943.

Soldier from
the 1ᵉʳ Régiment de France
incorporated in the FFI.

The Infantry and the FFI *(Forces Françaises de l'Intérieur)*

Pommiès Free Corps
(Corps Franc)
in the Vosges, 1944.

Officer in the Pommiès
Free Corps, in the Vosges,
1944.

FFI soldier 1944.

FFI soldier 1944.

RI (Infantry Regiment)
completely reconstituted
and British-equipped.

The Infantry

Corporal in the 27ᵉ RI (Infantry Regiment) in 1945. Regimental insignia, arm lozenge with Corporal's stripes, insignia of the 4ᵉ DMM (*Division Marocaine de Montagne* – Moroccan Mountain Division), 1918 Légion d'Honneur fourragère.

Adjudant from the 21ᵉ RI in 1945 in battle-dress with regimental 1914-18 Médaille Militaire fourragère.

Soldier in the 43ᵉ RI (Infantry Regiment) in 1945. Regimental insignia, 43ᵉ RI lozenge and 1ʳᵉ Division Motorisée d'Infanterie insignia, 1914-18 Croix de Guerre fourragère.

Soldier from the 106ᵉ RI in 1945 wearing battle-dress, French equipment with model 36 cartridge pouches, MAS 36 rifle and Adrian helmet.

Soldier from the 152ᵉ RI in 1945. Regimental insignia (the Red Devils), Légion d'Honneur fourragère.

The Infantry

Infantry Major in around
1944.

Infantryman
in the 1ʳᵉ Armée.

Infantryman in the Vosges
during the winter
of 1944. He has kept
the 1926-model Adrian
helmet and is wearing US
clothing.

Infantryman at the time
of the landings in Provence.

Infantryman in the Vosges
during the winter of 1944.

The zouaves

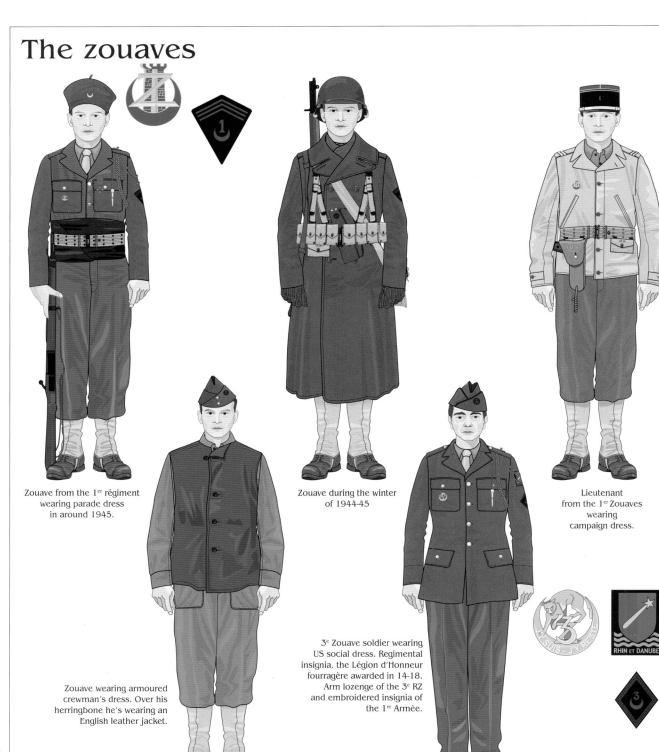

Zouave from the 1ᵉʳ régiment
wearing parade dress
in around 1945.

Zouave during the winter
of 1944-45

Lieutenant
from the 1ᵉʳ Zouaves
wearing
campaign dress.

Zouave wearing armoured
crewman's dress. Over his
herringbone he's wearing an
English leather jacket.

3ᵉ Zouave soldier wearing
US social dress. Regimental
insignia, the Légion d'Honneur
fourragère awarded in 14-18.
Arm lozenge of the 3ᵉ RZ
and embroidered insignia of
the 1ʳᵉ Armée.

The tirailleurs

Sergeant from the 1er RTA
in 1943
in North Africa.

Lieutenant from the 8e
RTM in Italy in 1944. On
his left sleeve
he is wearing
the embroidered
insignia and the
regimental lozenge.

Soldier from a Tirailleur
regiment wearing herringbone
overalls during the Provence
landings.

4e RTM soldier during
the winter of 1944-45.
He has kept the former
collar tabs of the 1935
French uniform and kept the
African troops'
Adrian helmet.

Sergeant in the 6e RTM
wearing parade dress in
1945.

17

The Mountain Infantry

99ᵉ RIA (Régiment d'Infanterie Alpine – Mountain Infantry Regiment) infantryman in 1944, ex-maquis from the Loire, wearing a *Chantier de jeunesse* tunic.

99ᵉ RIA infantryman in around 1944.

Ski scouts section soldier wearing reversible white clothing.

Scout section soldier wearing a reversible tunic.

Corporal from a scout section; he is wearing the brevet on his left sleeve.

The gendarmerie territoriale

Gendarme wearing heavy
cotton (summer) uniform

Gendarme wearing campaign
dress

NCO wearing the blue
(winter) uniform.

Gendarme during
the Liberation of Paris,
August 1944.

Gendarme during
the Liberation of Paris,
August 1944.

The chasseurs à pied

FRANCE

Free French Chasseur
in Great-Britain, 1941.

Lieutenant in the Free
French Chasseurs
in Great-Britain, 1941.

Free French Chasseur in
manoeuvres dress
in Great-Britain, 1941.

Lieutenant from the 2e
Chasseur, commanding
an FFI section in 1944.

Chasseur wearing US
dress in 1944.

The commandos d'Afrique

Commando wearing light US clothing.

Commando wearing US soldiers' waterproof.

NCO during Operation *Dragoon* in August 1944. He is armed with the Garand M1 rifle and equipped with a portable SCR 536 radio.

Officer during the 19 April 1945 parade in Paris.

Shoulder title "FRANCE" worn on the left sleeve, and Commandos d'Afrique insignia.

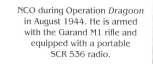

The chasseurs alpins

Mountain clothing
and white clothing
for the skier-scout sections.
These uniforms had
already been worn during
the Narvik Expedition in 1940
and were to be used again
in the BCA (Batallion
de Chasseurs Alpins)
units fighting
in the Alps in 1944.

The chasseurs alpins

As on the previous page, a variety of uniforms used on the Alps Front can be seen here. Note that the BCAs have held onto most of the French Model-36 equipment and the MAS 36 rifle. Likewise for the clothing which is still French.

The Foreign Legion

Legionnaire in the 13ᵉ DBLE in Libya in 1942.

Legionnaire wearing English heavy cotton clothing, with considerably shortened shorts.

Legionnaire wearing English heavy cotton clothing, but also wearing a French Colonial helmet, and is French-equipped and French-armed.

Corporal entirely re-equipped by the English.

Legionnaire in the 13ᵉ DBLE at Bir Hakeim, clothed by the English keeping the traditional white képi and his French equipment. Like his predecessors he is wearing the 1ʳᵉ DFL insignia on his left arm.

The Foreign Legion

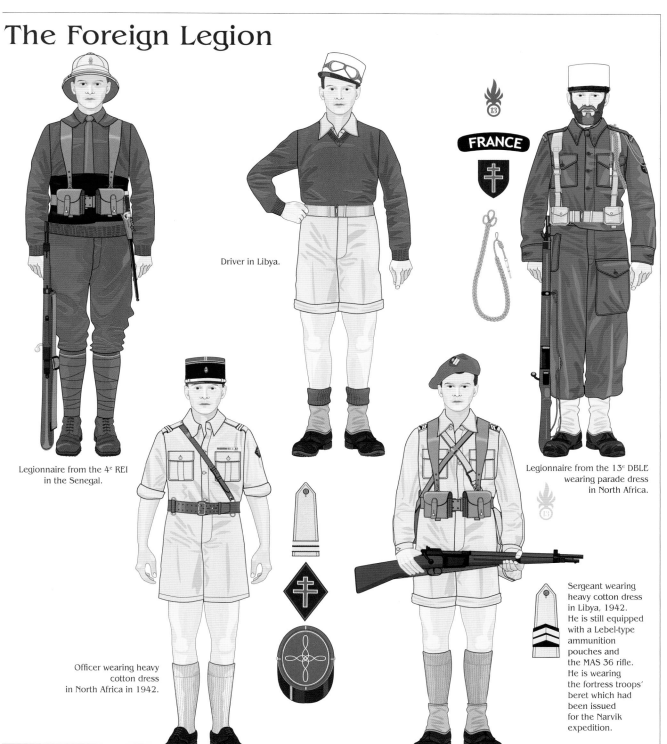

Driver in Libya.

FRANCE

Legionnaire from the 4ᵉ REI
in the Senegal.

Officer wearing heavy
cotton dress
in North Africa in 1942.

Legionnaire from the 13ᵉ DBLE
wearing parade dress
in North Africa.

Sergeant wearing
heavy cotton dress
in Libya, 1942.
He is still equipped
with a Lebel-type
ammunition
pouches and
the MAS 36 rifle.
He is wearing
the fortress troops'
beret which had
been issued
for the Narvik
expedition.

The Foreign Legion

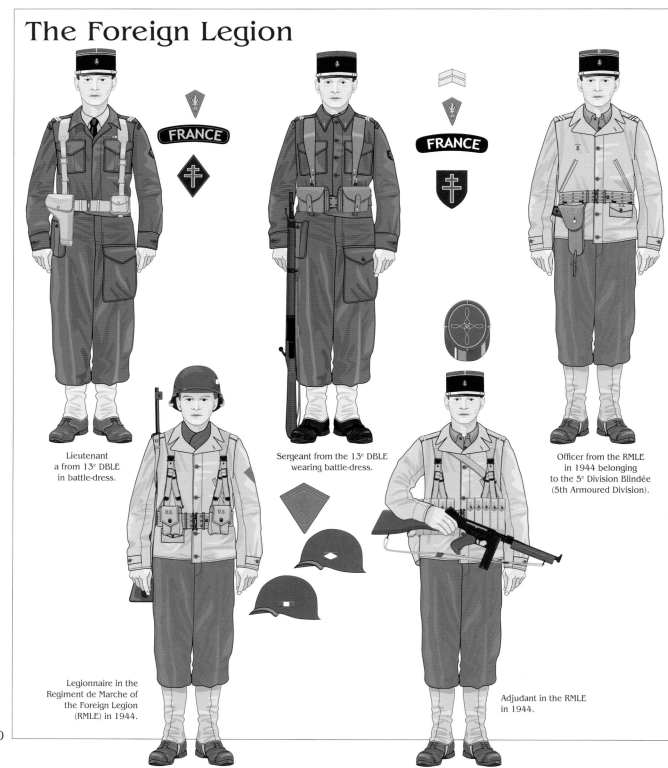

Lieutenant
a from 13e DBLE
in battle-dress.

Sergeant from the 13e DBLE
wearing battle-dress.

Officer from the RMLE
in 1944 belonging
to the 5e Division Blindée
(5th Armoured Division).

Legionnaire in the
Regiment de Marche of
the Foreign Legion
(RMLE) in 1944.

Adjudant in the RMLE
in 1944.

The Foreign Legion

Legionnaire from the RMLE
wearing combat dress.

Medic.

Legionnaire in the RMLE
wearing parade dress in 1944.

Legionnaire from the RMLE
wearing battle-dress.

Adjudant
in the 1er Régiment
Etranger de Cavalerie
wearing herringbone
overalls. Next to this,
the arm lozenge
of the 1er REC.

RHIN ET DANUBE

RMLE

The goumiers

Goumier wearing US dress
and a jellaba, and wearing
an English helmet
during the winter
in Italy.

Goumier in battle-dress
and a jellaba, wearing
a chechia on his head.

Goumier in battle-dress
and local shoes,
French-equipped
with a 92 carbine.

Sergent-chef.

Adjudant.

The goumiers

Adjudant's and Captain's kepis.

Sergeant from the 2ᵉ Tabor.

Mounted Captain. The harness
is the regulation issue
of the French pre-war cavalry.

Le 501ᵉ régiment de chars de combat

(RCC – Combat Tank Regiment)

Lieutenant wearing British dress in Africa in 1942.

Insignia of the 501ᵉ RCC.

Maréchal des logis chef in Africa in 1942.

Lieutenant from the 501 wearing battle-dress.

Tank crewman wearing herringbone dress.

Lieutenant from the 501ᵉ RCC incorporated into the 2ᵉ DB in 1944.

Le 501ᵉ régiment de chars de combat

(RCC – Combat Tank Regiment)

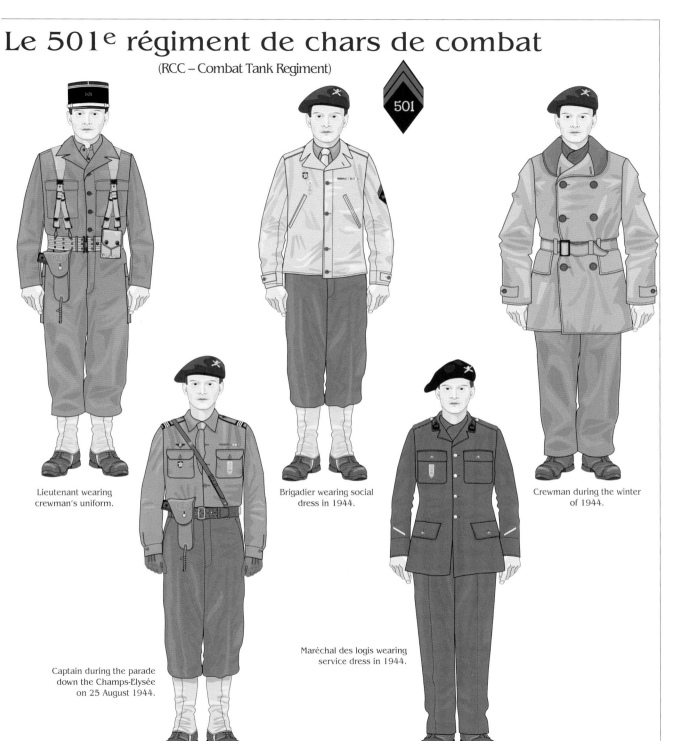

Lieutenant wearing crewman's uniform.

Brigadier wearing social dress in 1944.

Crewman during the winter of 1944.

Captain during the parade down the Champs-Elysée on 25 August 1944.

Maréchal des logis wearing service dress in 1944.

The cuirassiers, the dragoons

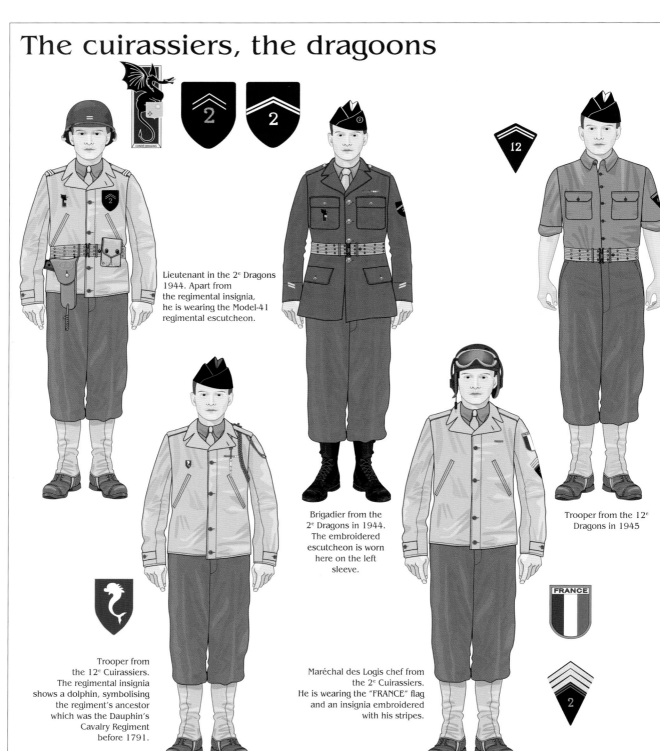

Lieutenant in the 2ᵉ Dragons 1944. Apart from the regimental insignia, he is wearing the Model-41 regimental escutcheon.

Brigadier from the 2ᵉ Dragons in 1944. The embroidered escutcheon is worn here on the left sleeve.

Trooper from the 12ᵉ Dragons in 1945

Trooper from the 12ᵉ Cuirassiers. The regimental insignia shows a dolphin, symbolising the regiment's ancestor which was the Dauphin's Cavalry Regiment before 1791.

Maréchal des Logis chef from the 2ᵉ Cuirassiers. He is wearing the "FRANCE" flag and an insignia embroidered with his stripes.

The chasseurs d'Afrique

Captain from the 5ᵉ RCA in
North Africa in 1942-43

Brigadier in the 5ᵉ RCA
in about 1942-43

Captain from the 12ᵉ RCA
in around 1942
during a parade.

Lieutenant wearing winter
clothing in around 1944.

Lieutenant from
the 8ᵉ RCA in about 1944.

The chasseurs d'Afrique

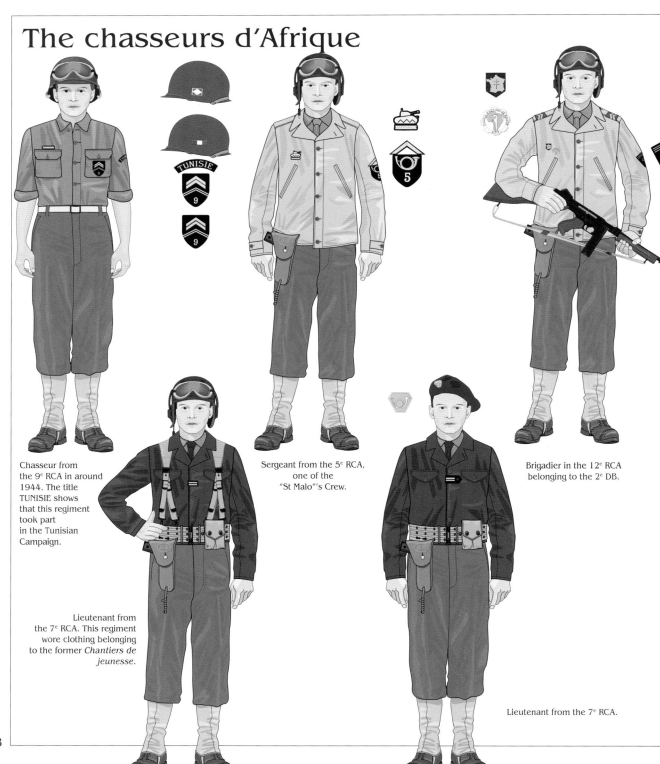

Chasseur from the 9ᵉ RCA in around 1944. The title TUNISIE shows that this regiment took part in the Tunisian Campaign.

Sergeant from the 5ᵉ RCA, one of the "St Malo"'s Crew.

Brigadier in the 12ᵉ RCA belonging to the 2ᵉ DB.

Lieutenant from the 7ᵉ RCA. This regiment wore clothing belonging to the former *Chantiers de jeunesse.*

Lieutenant from the 7ᵉ RCA.

The chasseurs d'Afrique

Sous-lieutenant in the 5ᵉ RCA in Germany, 1945.

Chasseur, 1st Class in the 5ᵉ RCA, one of the "Vouzier"'s crew, wearing social dress.

Chasseur, 1st Class in the 5ᵉ RCA wearing herringbone overalls.

Lieutenant from the 12ᵉ RCA during a parade in 1944.

Brigadier wearing parade dress during the Liberation of Paris.

The spahis

The first uniform for the recruits joining the 3ᵉ RMSM in 1944.

Brigadier from the 3ᵉ RMSM in 1944.

Lieutenant from the 3ᵉ RMSM wearing summer clothing.

Colonel of the 3ᵉ RSA (Régiment de Spahis Algériens) wearing the US herringbone tank suit, 1944.

Maréchal des Logis from the 5ᵉ RMSM during the 19 April 1945 parade. Note that the US tunic has been tucked into the trousers as was the tradition in the Armée d'Afrique.

The spahis

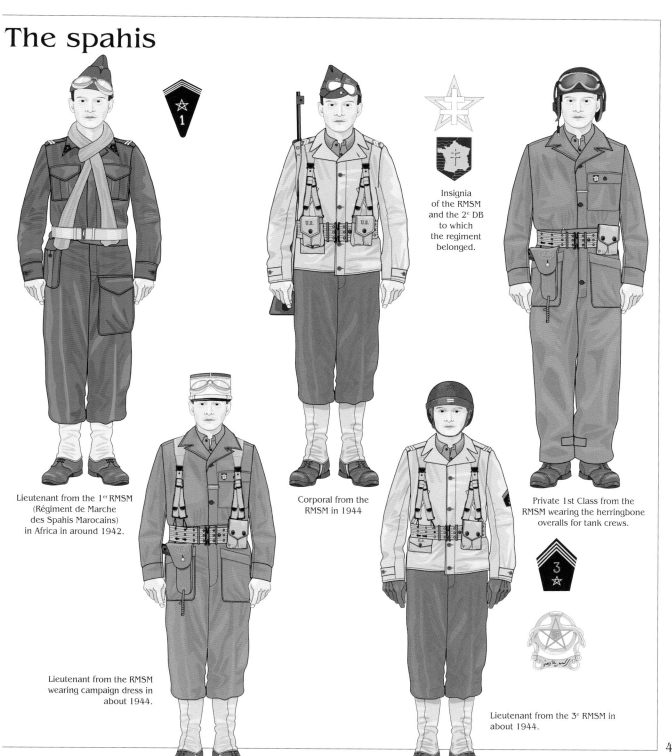

Lieutenant from the 1er RMSM
(Régiment de Marche
des Spahis Marocains)
in Africa in around 1942.

Insignia
of the RMSM
and the 2e DB
to which
the regiment
belonged.

Corporal from the
RMSM in 1944

Private 1st Class from the
RMSM wearing the herringbone
overalls for tank crews.

Lieutenant from the RMSM
wearing campaign dress in
about 1944.

Lieutenant from the 3e RMSM in
about 1944.

The Artillery

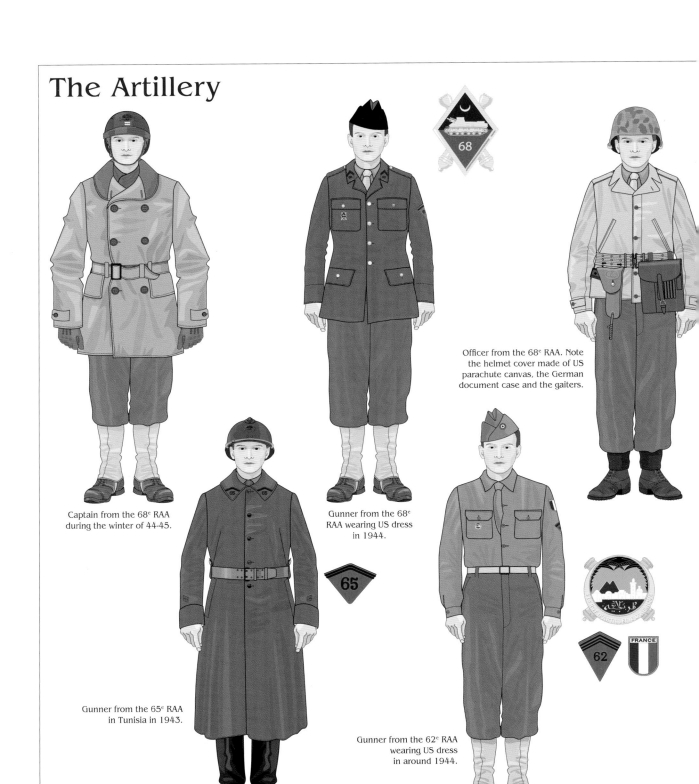

Captain from the 68ᵉ RAA during the winter of 44-45.

Gunner from the 65ᵉ RAA in Tunisia in 1943.

Gunner from the 68ᵉ RAA wearing US dress in 1944.

Gunner from the 62ᵉ RAA wearing US dress in around 1944.

Officer from the 68ᵉ RAA. Note the helmet cover made of US parachute canvas, the German document case and the gaiters.

The Artillery

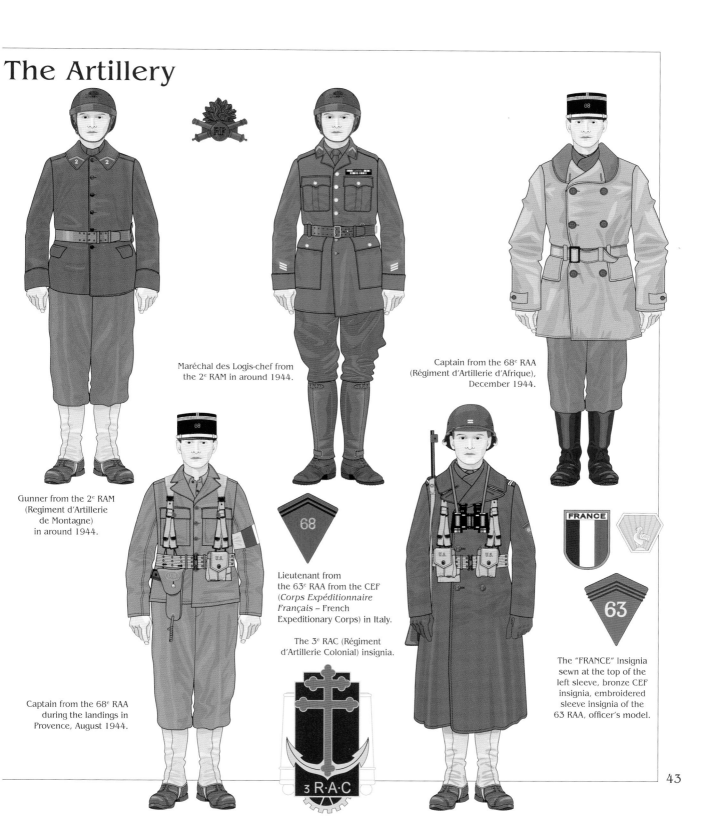

Gunner from the 2ᵉ RAM
(Regiment d'Artillerie
de Montagne)
in around 1944.

Maréchal des Logis-chef from
the 2ᵉ RAM in around 1944.

Captain from the 68ᵉ RAA
(Régiment d'Artillerie d'Afrique),
December 1944.

Captain from the 68ᵉ RAA
during the landings in
Provence, August 1944.

Lieutenant from
the 63ᵉ RAA from the CEF
(*Corps Expéditionnaire
Français* – French
Expeditionary Corps) in Italy.

The 3ᵉ RAC (Régiment
d'Artillerie Colonial) insignia.

The "FRANCE" Insignia
sewn at the top of the
left sleeve, bronze CEF
insignia, embroidered
sleeve insignia of the
63 RAA, officer's model.

The Engineers

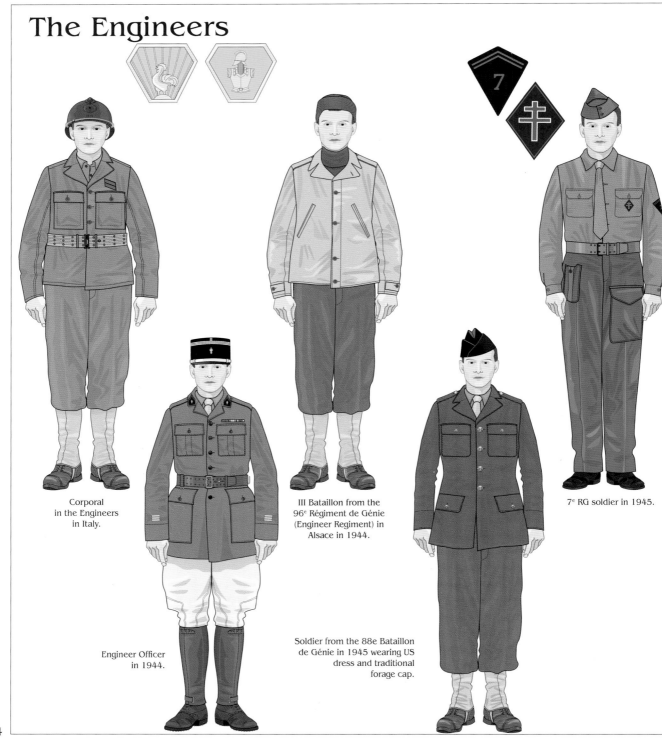

Corporal
in the Engineers
in Italy.

Engineer Officer
in 1944.

III Bataillon from the
96ᵉ Régiment de Génie
(Engineer Regiment) in
Alsace in 1944.

Soldier from the 88e Bataillon
de Génie in 1945 wearing US
dress and traditional
forage cap.

7ᵉ RG soldier in 1945.

The Army Health Service

FRANCE

Health Service driver from
the Feminine Ambulance
Section from the 7ᵉ RCA,
Italy in April 1944

Nurse wearing
service dress.

Medic in a North African
unit in Italy in 1944.

Captain-doctor in the FCM2
in Italy in 1944.

Lieutenant-doctor wearing
a US greatcoat from Hospital
422 in Italy in 1944.

49

The Colonial Troops

Colonial soldier from the Leclerc Column in around 1942.

Colonial wearing heavy cotton clothing in around 1942 with the Model-31 colonial helmet with a nationality insignia.

Colonial corporal from the Leclerc Column in 1942.

Lieutenant in battle-dress with the FFL lozenge on the left sleeve.

Lieutenant wearing heavy cotton clothing in around 1942.

The Colonial Troops

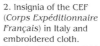

1
2

3

1. Nationality insignia
in bronze
2. Insignia of the CEF
(*Corps Expéditionnaire
Français*) in Italy and
embroidered cloth.
3. Embroidered model-41
insignia belonging
to the colonial troops.

Lieutenant wearing
parade dress in
North Africa around
1943. He is wearing
the 1941-Model
colonial troops'
insignia.

Colonial soldier
wearing US dress
during a parade at
Algiers in 1943.
He is wearing the
CEF insignia and
the colonial troops'
Model-41 escutcheon.

Colonial tank crewman
in around 1944.

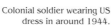

Colonial soldier wearing US
dress in around 1944.

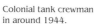

Colonial tank crewman
in around 1944.

The Colonial Troops

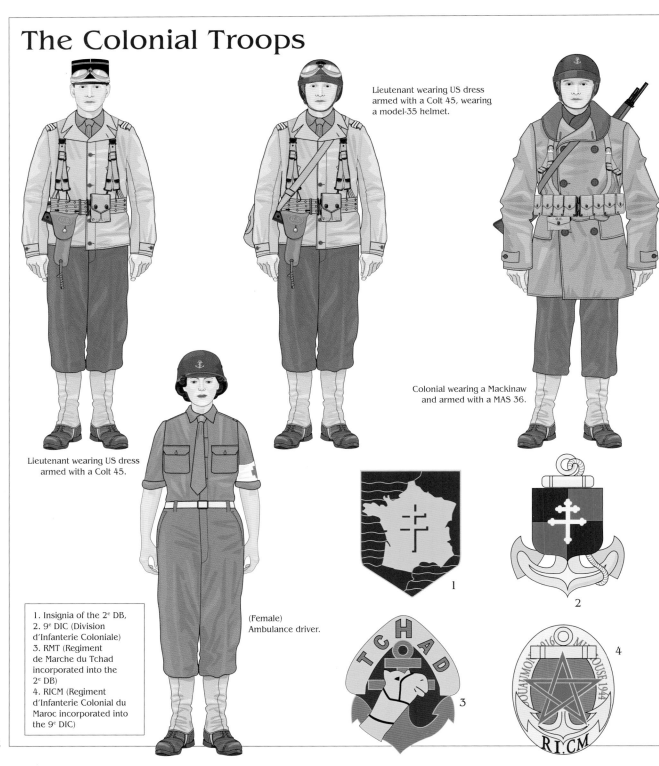

Lieutenant wearing US dress
armed with a Colt 45.

Lieutenant wearing US dress
armed with a Colt 45, wearing
a model-35 helmet.

Colonial wearing a Mackinaw
and armed with a MAS 36.

(Female)
Ambulance driver.

1. Insignia of the 2ᵉ DB,
2. 9ᵉ DIC (Division
d'Infanterie Coloniale)
3. RMT (Regiment
de Marche du Tchad
incorporated into the
2ᵉ DB)
4. RICM (Regiment
d'Infanterie Colonial du
Maroc incorporated into
the 9ᵉ DIC)

1

2

3

4

The Senegalese tirailleurs

Goumier Corporal in the Borkou nomad group in 1942. Note the Spahi cartridge pouches for cavalry carbines.

Sahara soldier 1942

Tirailleur wearing canvas dress in around 1942.

Bugler wearing canvas dress.

Corporal wearing a cardigan.

The Senegalese tirailleurs

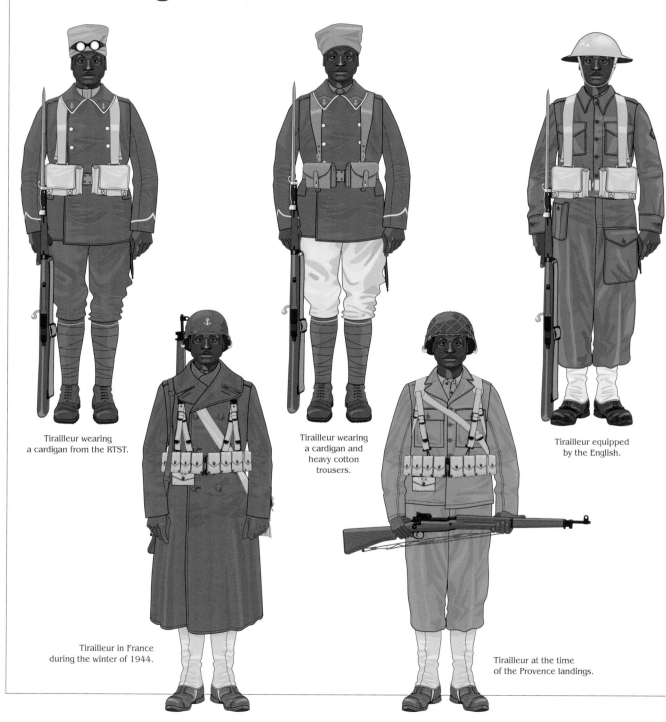

Tirailleur wearing
a cardigan from the RTST.

Tirailleur wearing
a cardigan and
heavy cotton
trousers.

Tirailleur equipped
by the English.

Tirailleur in France
during the winter of 1944.

Tirailleur at the time
of the Provence landings.

The Paris Police

Gardien de la Paix
in arms during
the Liberation of Paris
in August 1944.

Gardien
de la Paix
in arms during
the Liberation
of Paris
in August 1944.

Gardien de la Paix cyclist
or "Hirondelle" (*Swallow*)
in arms during the Liberation
of Paris in August 1944.

Police Brigadier.

Inspecteur-Principal in full dress
during the parade
for the Liberation of Paris.

The Armée de l'air (Air Force)

Pilot-Sergeant in the FAFL
(*Force Aérienne Française
Libre*) in 1941.

Pilot-Lieutenant
with both French
and English brevets
in around 1942.

NCO mechanic
in England
in around 1941.

Lieutenant-Chief Mechanic
from the Alsace Group
in Libya in 1942.

Lieutenant in the FAFL,
Alsace Group,
in Libya in 1942.

The Armée de l'air (Air Force)

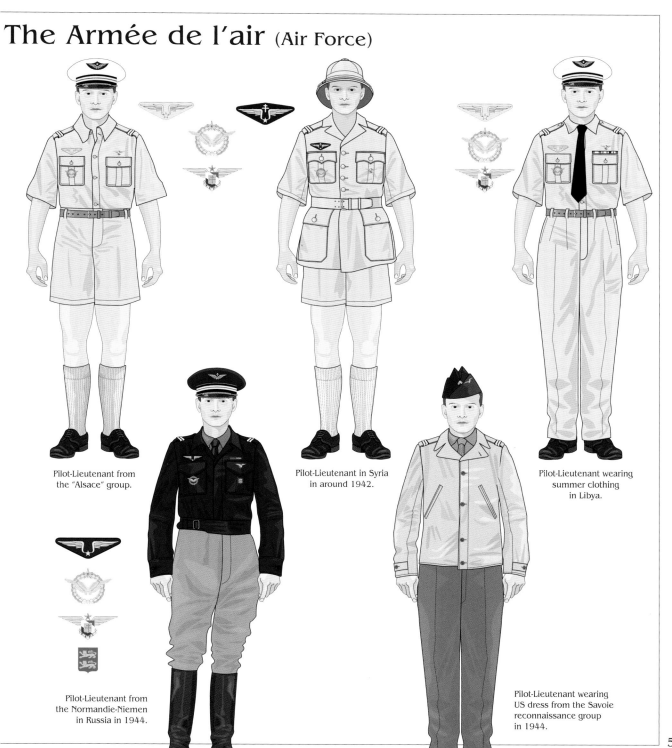

Pilot-Lieutenant from the "Alsace" group.

Pilot-Lieutenant in Syria in around 1942.

Pilot-Lieutenant wearing summer clothing in Libya.

Pilot-Lieutenant from the Normandie-Niemen in Russia in 1944.

Pilot-Lieutenant wearing US dress from the Savoie reconnaissance group in 1944.

The SAS (2ᵉ and 3ᵉ regiments de chasseurs parachutistes)

1. English parachute brevet.
2. SAS insignia.
3. Pegasus insignia of British Parachute Division.
4. FFL Parachute insignia.

WHO DARES WIN

Battle-dress.

Parachutist wearing British jump gear, 3ᵉ Bataillon d'Infanterie de l'Air in Brittany, 1944.

Commando uniform in North Africa.

The chasseurs parachutistes

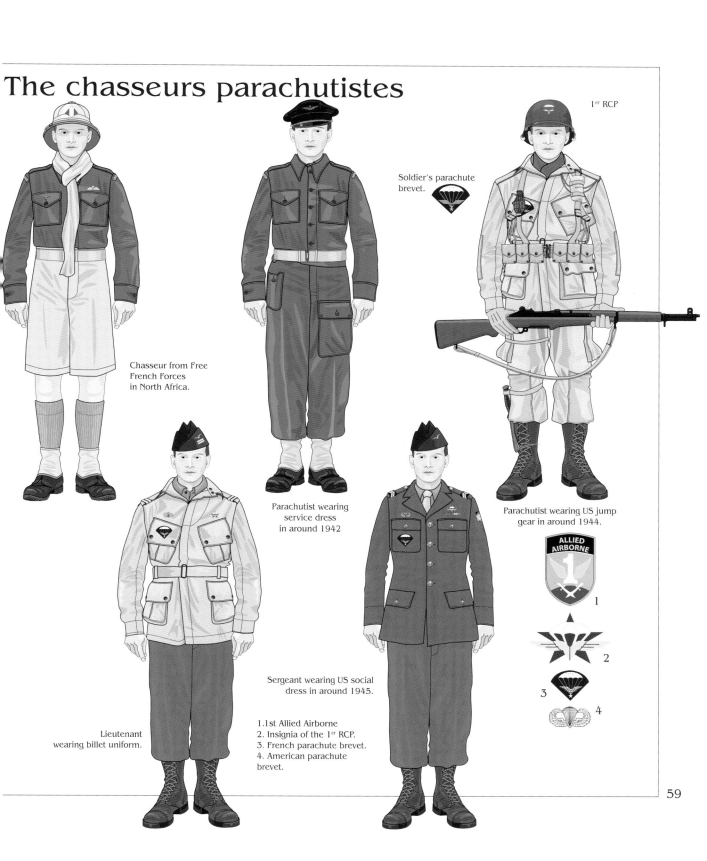

1er RCP

Soldier's parachute brevet.

Chasseur from Free French Forces in North Africa.

Parachutist wearing service dress in around 1942

Parachutist wearing US jump gear in around 1944.

Lieutenant wearing billet uniform.

Sergeant wearing US social dress in around 1945.

1. 1st Allied Airborne
2. Insignia of the 1er RCP.
3. French parachute brevet.
4. American parachute brevet.

ALLIED AIRBORNE 1

1

2

3

4

The chasseurs parachutistes (1er RCP)

Group commander

Gunner

Loader.

Suppliers.

The Forces Navales Françaises Libres
(Free French Navy)

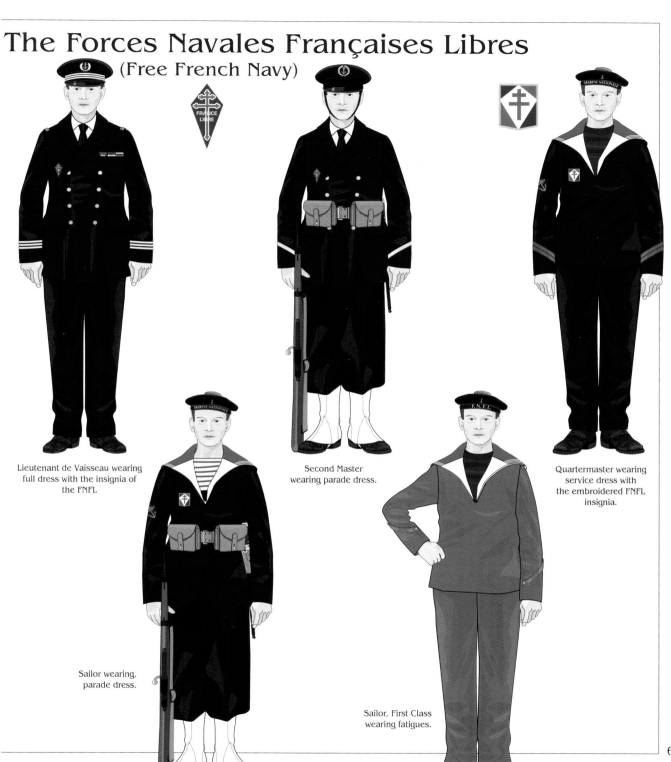

Lieutenant de Vaisseau wearing full dress with the insignia of the FNFL

Second Master wearing parade dress.

Quartermaster wearing service dress with the embroidered FNFL insignia.

Sailor wearing, parade dress.

Sailor, First Class wearing fatigues.

The Commandos Marine

FRANCE

N°4 COMMANDO

Embroidered FNFL shoulder
titles and insignia.

Sailor re-equipped
by the British in 1942.

Sailors wearing combat gear.
Loader, supplier
and gunner of a Bren gun.

Second-Master armed with
a Thompson sub-machine gun.

The Commandos Marine

Officer in British uniform,
wearing the green beret
of the British commandoes
with the FNFL escutcheon.

Copper insignia
of the Commandos Marines,

Embroidered sleeve insignia
of the British Commandoes.

Parade dress in
1944.

Combat dress at the time of the
Normandy landings
on 6 June 1944.
Note that the Commandos
Marines were the only French
troops to take part in Operation
Overlord, their objective being
the capture of Ouistreham.

1er Bataillon de FM
Commando, combat dress
in Holland, end of 1944.

The Fusiliers Marins (French Marines)

Fusiler-marin wearing
battle dress in around
1941.

Navy Officer wearing
battle dress
in around 1942.

Navy Officer in Libya
in 1942.

Quartermaster wearing
US dress in around 1944.

Second Master wearing
US parade dress
in around 1944
with an MAS 36 and
Lebel-type cartridge belts.

The Fusiliers Marins Regiments (RFM and RBFM)

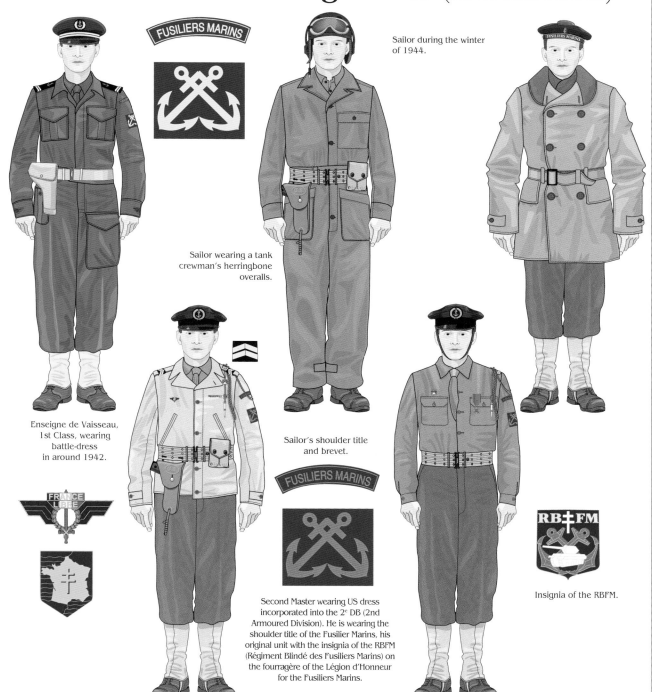

FUSILIERS MARINS

Sailor during the winter of 1944.

Sailor wearing a tank crewman's herringbone overalls.

Enseigne de Vaisseau, 1st Class, wearing battle-dress in around 1942.

Sailor's shoulder title and brevet.

FRANCE LIBRE

FUSILIERS MARINS

Second Master wearing US dress incorporated into the 2ᵉ DB (2nd Armoured Division). He is wearing the shoulder title of the Fusilier Marins, his original unit with the insignia of the RBFM (Régiment Blindé des Fusiliers Marins) on the fourragère of the Légion d'Honneur for the Fusiliers Marins.

RB✠FM

Insignia of the RBFM.

Bibliography

— *Militaria magazine* from the first issue.
— *L'uniforme and les armes des soldats de 1939-1945.*
L. and F. Funcken. Éditions Castermann
— Men at Arms n° 318 *l'Armée Française* de F. Vauvillier illustrations Mike Chappell. Osprey Publishing
— *Les chasseurs d'Afrique.* F. Vauvillier, colour plates by A. Jouineau. Éditions Histoire & Collections.
— *L'odyssée de la colonne Leclerc.* D. Corbonnois, A. Godec. Éditions Histoire & Collections
— *GI guide du Collectionneur,* H.-P. Enjames. Éditions Histoire & Collections.

Museum
— *Musée de l'Armée.* Hôtel des Invalides
— *Musée de l'Ordre de la Libération.* Hôtel des Invalides

Web Sites
— *Les Chasseurs de mémoire.*
— *Amicale de la Police.*

Design and layout Jean-Baptiste Mongin, André Jouineau
© Histoire & Collections 2012

ISBN: 978-2-35250-261-6
Publisher's number: 35250

Book edited by
HISTOIRE & COLLECTIONS
5, avenue de la République
F-75541 Paris Cedex 11 - FRANCE
Tel: +33-1 40 21 18 20
Fax: +33-1 47 00 51 11
www.histoireetcollections.com

This book has been designed, type laid-out and processed by Histoire Collections on fully integrated computer equipment

Color separation: Studio A &

Print by Pulsio SAR
European Union
November 20